MW01614788

I Think That
you're The
Bee's Knees!

# IT'S A KENTUCKY THING
## PART 2
## Y'ALL *STILL* WOULDN'T UNDERSTAND

Gumption
The Bee's Knees Cockamamie Courtin'
eener Than a Cutworm Monkey Suit
re You Raised in a Barn? Sundy Best
a Fiddle All Hat, No Cattle All Gommed Up
ce is Gonna Freeze Like That Cut a Shine
Up Goin' 'Muddin' Heavens to Betsy
t Like the Dickens Ain't No Count
Than a $2 Pistol Heavens to Betsy
Per Night Preachin' to the Choir
Out Tougher Than a Pine Knot
Really Gets My Goose
t in the Sam Hill?

**MICHAEL CRISP**

# It's a Kentucky Thing
## Part 2
### Y'all Still Wouldn't Understand

## By Michael Crisp

It's a Kentucky Thing, Part 2:
Y'all Still Wouldn't Understand

by Michael Crisp

Copyright © 2019

1st Edition cover & layout design by Kevin Kifer
www.k2-technology.com

ISBN 978-164669177-7

First Edition

Author Website
www.MICHAELCRISPONLINE.com

Published in Georgetown, KY
Printed in the U.S.A

# DEDICATION

To Kentucky's coal miners, as well as
your families, for your hard work,
determination, and pride in what you do.

- Michael Crisp

# About This Book

It's always a good idea to listen to your wife.

As you may remember from a story that I shared in my last book, the whole "Kentucky expressions" idea came from my wife, Anne Huber Crisp. She thought it would be a great idea for me to write a book that explored the wonderfully unique sayings that we hear while growing up in the Bluegrass state. Like a dutiful husband, I took her advice and the result was *It's a Kentucky Thing: Y'all Wouldn't Understand.*

Writing it was fun, but we had no idea it would become the sensation that it would be. Practically everyone across Kentucky embraced the book and felt personal connections to the classic sayings that were contained within, such as "over yonder," "I reckon," and "bless your heart."

When the book debuted, a media tour followed, which allowed me to appear on various television stations to promote the book. These interviews, which included appearances in Lexington on WKYT (CBS), WTVQ (ABC) and WLEX (NBC) were a treat, but I probably had the most fun during an hourlong radio interview that I did on Jack Pattie's morning show.

Jack Pattie has been a fixture in the radio scene for several years, and he is the longtime host of a popular weekday morning show on WVLK in Lexington. He invited me onto his show to discuss my book, and during our interview he took calls from his listeners so they could share on air some of their favorite expressions that they heard growing up. We had a blast talking with callers and hearing their favorite expressions - some of which happened to be in my book. Quite a few of their sayings not only weren't in my book, I also hadn't heard of them before. It was both fun and fascinating to learn about these sayings. One caller mentioned that his grandmother used to say "I'll let you get back to your rat killin'" whenever she would say goodbye to someone. Jack and had a good laugh about that one!

There's no doubt about it, *It's a Kentucky Thing: Y'all Wouldn't Understand* became one of the most enjoyable projects of my career. It's fun to reminisce about these old expressions, and you can't help but smile when you're thinking about them - or better yet, saying them to someone. And because there are so many great expressions out there, the decision to write a sequel an easy one.

When I was writing the first book, I researched over 300 expressions that were worthy of inclusion, but I wanted to whittle it down to just the top 100 expressions that I believed Kentuckians would know. This time around, I've chosen another 100 expressions for you that I'm sure you'll enjoy. And like last time, I've left some room in the back of the book for you to write down a few of your favorite Kentucky expressions as well.

Well, I guess that's enough out of me. I'll let you get back to your rat killin'!

# SOME OF OUR FAVORITE KENTUCKY WORDS

Most of this book is about our favorite phrases, but let's not forget about some of our favorite words that have their own unique, down home meaning here in Kentucky:

Buggy - shopping cart
Clicker - remote control for your TV
Bloomers - female underwear
Holler - a valley or ravine between mountains
Boonies - a remote, rural area
Polecat - skunk
Skift - a light dusting of snow
Tote - to carry or transport
Aimin' - planning to
Redneck - a rural, working-class person
Hillbilly - a rural, unsophisticated person
Jasper - an outsider or stranger
Young'un - a child or young adult
You'ns - you one's (similar to y'all)
Floozy - a woman of questionable reputation
Hogwash - nonsense or jibberish
Chaw - a piece of chewing tobacco
Passel - a large group or number
Rurnt - ruined
Sop - soak
Slop - leftover food you give your animals
Lightning bugs - firefly

# CRITERIA

The expressions you see in this book were chosen based on the following criteria:

First and foremost, I had to be familiar with the phrases and have had to had heard them at least once in my lifetime. Sure, most of the expressions in this book probably weren't invented in Kentucky, but it was important to me that they have been spoken by a Kentuckian at least a time or two.

Second, I gave preferential treatment to expressions that featured a combination of words rather than just one word. I made a few exceptions to this rule by including a handful of one-word expressions like cockamamie, whippersnapper, and courtin', but the vast majority of phrases in this book feature more than just one word.

Finally, the expressions needed to be timeless and unforgettable. These southern sayings have been around for generations, and it's important that future generations of Kentuckians continue to use them for years to come. They've stood the test of time, not it's up to us to keep 'em around for as long as we can.

So quit your lollygaggin'. It's time to get started!

# #1

# "What's Good for the Goose is Good for the Gander"

If a man can do it, a woman can do it too.

*"You're out every night with the boys but you don't want me to go out with my girlfriends? Well, what's good for the goose is good for the gander!"*

This phrase is a variation of "what's sauce for the goose is sauce for the gander," which was described by author John Ray as a "woman's proverb" in his book *A Collection of English Proverbs*. The saying traces its roots to cooking, as it was commonplace to use the same type of sauce when serving either goose or gander (a male goose) for dinner. Incidentally, this isn't the only time "gander" appears in a famous Kentucky phrase. "Take a gander" means "to stretch one's neck to see" - much like a goose!

***Now that really gets my goose!***

*courtesy of Wikipedia*

# #2

# "The Bee's Knees"

## DEFINITION

Someone or something that's great or wonderful.

## EXAMPLE

*"We had flapjacks and bacon and the kids thought their breakfast was the bee's knees."*

## SIMILAR EXPRESSIONS

"The cat's meow"
"The cat's ass"

# #3

# "Gettin' too Big for His Britches"

## DEFINITION

Someone who is conceited, cocky or prideful.

## EXAMPLE

*"Look at him walking around with his nose in the air. I swear that boy is getting' too big for his britches!"*

## ORIGIN

According to author Laura Lee, this saying is rooted in the old Scottish phrase "He thinks he's big, but a wee coat fits him." The first time the phrase was used in print however was when legendary frontiersman Davy Crockett wrote "I myself was one of the first to fire a gun under Andrew Jackson. I helped to give him all his glory. But I liked him well once: but when a man gets too big for his breeches, I say goodbye."

# #4

# "Keener Than a Cutworm"

## DEFINITION

Something that's really sharp.

## EXAMPLE

*"I wouldn't play with that pocketknife if I were you. The blade on it is keener than a cutworm."*

## FUN FACT

Cutworms aren't actually worms - they're moth caterpillars. These pesky critters hide in the soil and eat through plant stems, which can take a toll on the plants in your garden or flower bed.

# #5

# "Fit as a Fiddle'"

In excellent health.

*"My checkup went really well, because the doctor said I was fit as a fiddle!"*

The "Official Kentucky State Old-Time Fiddler's Contest" is an annual competition held each June in Elizabethtown, Kentucky.

**"Fit as a violin" just wouldn't make sense!**

*courtesy of Wikipedia*

# #6

# "Well I'll Be a Monkey's Uncle"

I'm shocked or surprised.

*"You mean to tell me that Ale 8 is making a cherry-flavored ginger ale? Well I'll be a monkey's uncle!"*

The phrase first gained popularity shortly after the famous Scopes Trial in 1925, especially by creationists who used it as a sarcastic retort to those who believed that man descended from apes.

# #7

# "Two Shakes of a Lamb's Tail"

## DEFINITION

A very short period of time.

## EXAMPLE

*"I'm on my way, don't worry - I'll be there in two shakes of a lamb's tail"*

## FUN FACT

The small community of Lamb, Kentucky is located in Monroe County. It even had its own post office (until 1994, when it closed).

# #8

# "All Hat, No Cattle"

## DEFINITION

Someone who is all talk but no action.

## EXAMPLE

*"That politician talks a big game but he's full of empty promises. He's all hat, no cattle."*

## FUN FACT

With over 2 million cattle in Kentucky, we are the 14th largest state in cattle population. That's something that we can brag about 'til the cows come home.

# #9

# "Fit to Be Tied"

## DEFINITION

Frustrated or angry.

## EXAMPLE

*"He thinks he can get away with smartin' off to me?
Lord have mercy, I'm fit to be tied!"*

## SIMILAR EXPRESSION

"I've about had it"
"I'm so mad I could spit"

# #10

# "Rustle Up Some Vittles"

## DEFINITION

Prepare food on short notice.

## EXAMPLE

*"You look awful hungry - why don't you have a seat and I'll rustle up some vittles for you."*

## ORIGIN

Rustle is an actual word that means "to make, find or prepare something quickly", and was used with some commonality in 1800s and 1900s. "Vittles" is a bit more obscure though, as it's derived from the word "victual", which means "food or provisions".

**Druther's Restaurant in Campbellsville, Kentucky**
*courtesy of Wikipedia*

# #11

# "If I Had My Druthers"

## DEFINITION

If it were up to me or if I could choose.

## EXAMPLE

*"If I had my druthers, I'd go golfing today instead of going to work."*

## FUN FACT

Druther's restaurants were a popular fast food chain in the 1980s. The last remaining Druthers restaurant that is still in business is located in Campbellsville, Kentucky.

# #12

# "Cockamamie"

## DEFINITION

Ridiculous or nonsensical.

## EXAMPLE

*"I'm tired of hearing your cockamamie stories!"*

## ORIGIN

Cockamamie comes from the decorating term décalcomanie, which gained popularity in France during the mid-19th century. Décalcomanie involved the use of transfers, or decals, to decorate furniture and other types of household items. By the 1920s, the concept made its way to America with candy companies giving away ink transfers and temporary tattoos with their products in order to better market their candy to a younger generation. American children, especially in and around Brooklyn, New York, shortened the word and changed its pronunciation to "cockamamie."

# #13

# "Whippersnapper"

## DEFINITION

A young or inexperienced person.

## EXAMPLE

*"You young whippersnappers wouldn't know a good Christmas tree if you saw one!"*

## ORIGIN

This word comes from a combination of the phrase "whip snapper", which means someone who doesn't possess a strong vocabulary, and "snipper snapper", which was a 17th century term for a street rogue.

# #14

# "Well, If That Don't Beat All"

That's amazing.

*"You mean to tell me that Emily showed up to work on time? Well, if that don't beat all!"*

"That takes the cake"
"Well slap my mama"
"Well slap my head and call me silly"

# #15

# "Goin' Muddin'"

Driving your truck or other type of 4x4 vehicle off road in the mud.

*"We're goin' muddin' this weekend and I can't wait!"*

Mud Dauber wasps like to use mud to build their huts.

*If you think these two are goin' muddin', you're probably right!*

*courtesy of Wikipedia*

# #16

# "Get Turned Around"

## DEFINITION

To become lost.

## EXAMPLE

*"I hate drivin' over in Frankfort, I always get turned around."*

## FUN FACT

A 22-month old toddler survived in the woods for 3 days after being lost near his home in Magoffin County, Kentucky.

# #17

# "Quit Your Bellyachin'"

## DEFINITION

Stop complaining.

## EXAMPLE

*"Quit your bellyachin' about the traffic, we'll get to Mama's in time for supper."*

## SIMILAR EXPRESSION

"Won't you just hush"
"Put a sock in it"
"Shut your trap"
"Shut your pie hole"

# #18

# "On the Draw"

### DEFINITION

A person receiving compensation for a work-related injury.

### EXAMPLE

*"Frank ain't hurtin' for money, he's been on the draw since last year."*

### FUN FACT

Kentucky's first Workman's Compensation Act was introduced in 1914 but was rejected after it was declared unconstitutional.

# #19

# "Richer Than 3 Feet Up a Bull's Ass"

## DEFINITION

Very wealthy.

## EXAMPLE

*"Elmer buys a brand new Cadillac every year 'cause he's richer than 3 feet up a bull's ass."*

## SIMILAR EXPRESSION

"Richer than Croesus"
"So rich he buys a new boat when his other one gets wet"

# #20

# "Like the Dickens'"

## DEFINITION

Like the devil

## EXAMPLE

*"It's hotter than the dickens in the house, turn on the damn air conditioner!"*

## ORIGIN

'Dickens' isn't actually a reference to the author Charles Dickens. It's an old euphemism meaning "the devil", and it's been around for a while. William Shakespeare used the phrase in his play *The Merry Wives of Windsor* back in 1600 when he wrote "I cannot tell what the dickens his name is my husband had him of."

*It hurts like the dickens to know Charles Dickens didn't have anything to do with this phrase.*

courtesy of Wikipedia

# #21

# "Sunday-Go-to-Meetin' Clothes"

## DEFINITION

You best church outfit.

## EXAMPLE

*"You can't wear a t-shirt to court, Ernie. Go put on your Sunday-go-to-meetin' clothes!"*

## SIMILAR EXPRESSION

"Sundy best"
"All gussied up"

# #22

# "Ain't No Count"

| DEFINITION |
|---|

Worthless.

| EXAMPLE |
|---|

*"Oh, don't listen to John, he ain't no count."*

| FUN FACT |
|---|

If you counted all of the miles that have already been explored in Mammoth Cave, that number would be 400.

# #23

# "Don't Count Your Chickens Before They Hatch"

---
**DEFINITION**
---

Don't make plans based on a prediction.

---
**EXAMPLE**
---

*"You haven't been hired yet Becky, so don't start spending your money. Don't count your chickens before they hatch!"*

---
**ORIGIN**
---

In Aesop's fable *The Milkmaid and Her Pail*, the milkmaid daydreams of selling the milk she is carrying, which will lead to her becoming wealthy and attracting a husband. She stumbles and drops the milk and her aspirations are lost. This leads to her mother telling her "Do not count your chickens before they are hatched." Wise words indeed, thanks Aesop!

# #24

# "Put On Airs"

## DEFINITION

To appear superior to other people.

## EXAMPLE

*"Take off that tuxedo right now! We're just going to Red Lobster, there's no need to put on airs!"*

## ORIGIN

We can thank the French again for this one. "Air" comes from the French word "air" which means "look, appearance or bearing." Since the 16th century the phrase "put on airs" has meant to describe people who think that they are better than everyone else, or at the very least act like it.

# #25

# "You Sound Just Like a Broken Record"

## DEFINITION

You are being annoyingly repetitive.

## EXAMPLE

*"I'll give you an answer tomorrow, so quit asking me. You sound just like a broken record!"*

## FUN FACT

Six years after he invented the phonograph, Thomas Edison debuted his incandescent light bulb at the Southern Exposition in Louisville in 1883.

# #26

# "Playin' Possum"

To pretend to be asleep or dead.

*"Ricky, I know you can hear me - quit playin' possum and go out there and mow the yard!"*

This phrase references the opossum, a small animal who sometimes pretends to be dead when they encounter predators.

# #27

# "Walking-Around Money"

## DEFINITION

pocket money that is carried for everyday expenditures.

## EXAMPLE

*"He's got him a wad of walkin'-around money that's burnin' a hole in his pocket!"*

## ORIGIN

The earliest known account of the phrase happened in an Irish bankruptcy court when a man named Barney Eastwood asked the judge presiding over his hearing for some "walking about money." In 20th century American politics, however, "walking-around money" generally means bribe money that candidates would hand out to their constituents in order to buy their votes on election day.

# #28

# "Slap Worn Out"

| DEFINITION |
|---|

Extremely tired.

| EXAMPLE |
|---|

*"I'm so slap worn out that I can barely keep my eyes open!"*

| SIMILAR EXPRESSION |
|---|

"Dog tired"
"Tired as all get out"
"Tired as a worn out shoe"

# #29

# "Nary a One"

Not a single one.

*"I invited all my friends to my Mary Kay party but nary a one showed up!"*

"Nary" is derived from "ne'er", which is a contraction of the word "never".

# #30

# "'Til the Cows Come Home"

For an extremely long period of time.

*"We can talk about it 'til the cows come home, but I'm not letting you go to that dance!"*

"'Til you're blue in the face"
"'til hell freezes over"
"That'll be the day"

# #31

# "If Wishes Were Fishes We'd All Have a Fry"

This phrase can trace its roots to an old Scottish nursery rhyme that says "If wishes were horses then beggars would ride, if turnips were swords I'd have one by my side. If 'ifs' and 'ands' were pots and pans there would be no need for tinker's hands!" This idiom has several other adaptions, including a 20th century American version that says "If 'ifs' and 'buts' were candy and nuts we'd all have a merry Christmas!"

# #32

# "Actin' Like a Heathen Child"

## DEFINITION

Behaving wildly or out of control.

## EXAMPLE

*"He's runnin' through the house screamin' actin' like a damn heathen child!"*

## ORIGIN

A 'heathen' is a person who doesn't belong to a traditional religion, such as Christianity, or someone who acts in an immoral way. If you were a rambunctious child, your mother (or grandmother) probably called you a heathen a time or two!

***This little guy is livin' high on the hog.***

*courtesy of Wikipedia*

# #33

# "Livin' High on the Hog"

## DEFINITION

To prosper or live well.

## EXAMPLE

*"Once they put that highway in next to our store we'll be livin' high on the hog!"*

## ORIGIN

Traditionally, the choicest cuts of a pig can be found on its back and upper leg. Usually the wealthy would eat "high on the hog" while paupers could only afford the belly pork and feet.

# #34

# "All Gommed Up"

Not functioning due to a clog or a mess.

*"Rinse the food off those dirty dishes or you'll gom up the dishwasher for sure!"*

A gom, or sometimes spelled "gaum", is a derivative of "gum" - which alludes to a sticky substance that can create a mess or a problem.

# #35

# "We're Gonna Have Us a Hootenanny (or Humdinger)"

## DEFINITION

An informal party, usually with music.

## EXAMPLE

*"In that case a celebration is in order. We're gonna have us a hootenanny!"*

## SIMILAR EXPRESSION

"Shindig"

# #36

# "Built Like a Brick Shithouse"

## DEFINITION

Having a curvy figure (for a female) or strong physique (for a male).

## EXAMPLE

*"I'm old and skinny now, but I was built like a brick shithouse back in the day!"*

## ORIGIN

This saying may be one of the earliest examples of "toilet humor". Before the advent of indoor plumbing, outhouses were used when you needed to go to the bathroom. Outhouses weren't very sturdy, as they were typically constructed out of old wood planks. Kentucky's last remaining functioning outhouse is located at Penn's Grocery in Gravel Switch, Kentucky.

# #37

# "Turn Tail and Run"

## DEFINITION

Run away or flee.

## EXAMPLE

*"Those bandits decided to turn tail and run once they heard the police sirens."*

## SIMILAR EXPRESSIONS

"Hot-tail it out of there"
"Get while the gettin's good"

# #38

# "Well, I S'wanee"

Well, I swear.

*"Well, I s'wanee I don't know what you're talking about."*

This phrase dates back a few decades when Stephen Foster, composer of the famous song "My Old Kentucky Home, Goodnight", authored the song "Old Folks at Home". In the song, Foster references the Suwannee River, which runs from southern Georgia through Florida and empties out to the Gulf of Mexico. In his song he calls it the "Swanee Ribber", however, and this shortened phrase stuck around for a while. In the 1930s, singer Al Jolson had a hit record in 1920 with the song "Swanee", which was so popular at the time that southerners began working the term into conversation. Before long, "I s'wanee" became a generally accepted substitute for saying "I swear".

# #39

# "Actin' Like the Queen of Sheba"

## DEFINITION

Acting very self-important.

## EXAMPLE

*"Well look at her, actin' all high and mighty like the Queen of Sheba!"*

## ORIGIN

In the Bible, the Queen of Sheba travels to Jerusalem to meet with King Solomon in order to receive his counsel. In the story, the Queen bestows lavish gifts on King Solomon, praises the wisdom she has received from him, and returns home to Jerusalem.

# #40

# "Tighter Than Dick's Hatband"

## DEFINITION

Very miserly or greedy.

## EXAMPLE

*"Bruce ain't gonna loan you any money, he's tighter than Dick's headband!"*

## SIMILAR EXPRESSIONS

"Tighter than the bark on a tree"
"tighter than a bull's ass"
"Tighter than a flea's ass over a rain barrel"

# #41

# "A Good Lickin'"

## DEFINITION

To beat an opponent in a fight or a game.

## EXAMPLE

*"You make that face at me again and I'm gonna give you a good lickin'."*

## FUN FACT

Legendary frontiersman Davy Crockett is often credited with giving a speech in which he said "I'm half-horse, half-alligator and a little attached with snapping turtle. I've got the fastest horse, the prettiest sister, the surest rifle and the ugliest dog in Texas. My father can lick any man in Kentucky - and I can lick my father." This quote actually comes from an 1831 play by James Kirke Paulding called *The Lion of the West* which features a character named Colonel Nimrod Wildfire, who was based on Crockett.

# #42

# "Monkey Suit"

## DEFINITION

A tuxedo or uniform.

## EXAMPLE

*"I can't wait to get out of this monkey suit and back in my normal clothes."*

## ORIGIN

This term came about in the 1820s and was originally "monkey jacket". It likened a uniform, tuxedo or tight-fitting dress clothing to the type of jacket normally worn by an organ grinder's monkey.

# #43

# "Their Cornbread Ain't Done in the Middle"

A description for a person who lacks common sense.

*"Don't listen to a word he says - his cornbread ain't done in the middle."*

"They ain't right"
"They only have one oar in the water"
"Their brain rattles around like a BB in a boxcar"

*There's a lot of bang for your buck with a $2 pistol.*

*courtesy of Wikipedia*

# #44

# "Hotter Than a $2 Pistol"

## DEFINITION

Something that has been stolen (or attractive/sexy).

## EXAMPLE

*"Lord have mercy, that girl is hotter than a $2 pistol on the 4th of July!"*

## ORIGIN

In the early part of the 20th century, it was possible to purchase a cheap handgun for around $2. Despite their affordable price, these firearms (sometimes called "Saturday night specials") were often stolen and pawned, earning them a reputation for being carried and used by criminals.

# #45

# "You Can't Make a Silk Purse Out of a Sow's Ear"

You can't turn something that's worthless into something of value.

*"You think slappin' a coat of paint on that old truck is gonna make it run better? You can't make a silk purse out of a sow's ear!"*

There is a town called Pig that's located in southern Edmonson County, Kentucky, about 20 miles away from Bowling Green.

# #46

# "Pretty Per Night"

A woman who frequently goes out to socialize, typically to draw attention from men.

*"Look at her getting' all dolled up again to hit the town. Talk about being a pretty per night!"*

Kentucky women are the most beautiful (inside and out) in the world!

# #47

# "They've Got a Good Turn"

# #48

# "A Bunch of Malarkey"

---

## DEFINITION

Meaningless talk or nonsense.

---

## EXAMPLE

*"The more he talks, the more I realize what he's saying is just a bunch of malarkey!"*

---

## SIMILAR EXPRESSIONS

"Hogwash"
"Guff"
"Jibberish"
"Bullshit"
"Bull hockey"
"Balderdash"

# #49

# "Cut a Shine"

## DEFINITION

To make a positive impression on someone, usually by showing off.

## EXAMPLE

*"With all his singing and dancing, Bobby sure is cuttin' a shine with Missy right now."*

## ORIGIN

This phrase originates from the idiom "cutting a head shine," which means "to pull off a trick or a caper in an entertaining way."

# #50

# "Quit Pissin' and Moanin' About It"

## DEFINITION

Stop complaining.

## EXAMPLE

*"I'm taking you to the dentist whether you like it or not, so quit pissin' and moanin' about it."*

## FUN FACT

If you're moanin' while you're pissin', you may have a urinary tract infection and should see a doctor.

# #51

# "Dumber Than a Box of Rocks"

## DEFINITION

Very stupid.

## EXAMPLE

*"Jill can't help you with your math homework because she's dumber than a box of rocks."*

## ORIGIN

"Dumber than a bag of hammers"
"Dumb as shit"
"Dumbass"
"Dumb as hell"

# #52

# "As All Get Out"

## DEFINITION

To the extreme.

## EXAMPLE

*"This book is as funny as all get out!"*

## ORIGIN

"All get out" is actually a tamer version of saying "hell." The first time that this phrase appeared in print was in Mark Twain's 1884 book *Huckleberry Finn*, when Tom Sawyer warns "We ain't got no time to bother of that. We got to dig in like all git-out."

# #53

# "The Devil is Beating His Wife"

## DEFINITION

The sun is shining while it's raining.

## EXAMPLE

*"I don't know where all the clouds went, but this rain sure feels good in the summer sun. I guess the devil's beating his wife right now."*

## ORIGIN

Although this saying that describes a sunshower has been around a while, it first appeared in print in *The Book of Woodcraft* and *Indian Lore* by Ernest Thompson Seton. Other variations of this phrase include "the Devil is whipping his wife" and "the Devil is chasing his wife." All of these examples beg the obvious question "who would ever want to marry the Devil?"

# #54

# "It Don't Amount to a Hill of Beans"

Something that's worthless or worth very little.

*"The problems of two little people don't amount to a hill of beans in this world."*

If you're from Kentucky you've probably eaten soup beans and cornbread at least once or twice, maybe even with a side of chow-chow.

# #55

# "My Back Teeth Are Floating"

# #56

# "As Pretty as a Peach"

| DEFINITION |
|---|

Adorable.

| EXAMPLE |
|---|

*"Have you seen Carla's daughter? Well she's just pretty as a peach!"*

| FUN FACT |
|---|

Peach trees can be found throughout Kentucky, especially in the western part of the state where conditions are a bit more ideal for their growth.

# #57

# "Heavens to Betsy"

An exclamation of mild surprise.

*"You got an 'A' on your algebra? Heavens to Betsy, I'm so proud of you!"*

"Heavens to Betsy" was a popular 19th century American phrase, first appearing in print in an 1857 issue of *Ballou's Dollar Daily* magazine. Although it has been speculated that the saying references Betsy Ross, the identity of "Betsy" has never been officially confirmed.

**Not sure if 'Heavens to Betsy' is about Betsy Ross?**
**Sew what?**

*courtesy of Wikipedia*

# #58

# "Girded Up"

Wearing a girdle and bra.

*"You better get girded up before you try to squeeze into that dress."*

This saying originates from the phrase "gird up your loins," which appears occasionally in the Bible. In Biblical times, both men and women wore tunics - which were fastened around the waist by a belt or girdle. When it was time to do hard work or go to battle, men would "gird up" by tucking their tunic into their belt.

# #59

# "He Just Fell off the Turnip Truck"

## DEFINITION

Extremely naive.

## EXAMPLE

*"He'll believe anything you tell him. It's like he just fell off the turnip truck."*

## ORIGIN

As a cheap, bland-tasting root vegetable, turnips have often been associated with being a food that only poor people eat. In England, turnips were a crop that was often fed to pigs and sheep. Over the years, the insults "turnip-eater" and "turnip-head" came to pass, which were the equivalent of calling someone an idiot or a simpleton. By 1836, Charles Dickens used the word "turnip" in his *Pickwick Papers* when his character Sam Weller describes himself.

# #60

# "Quit Your Lollygagging"

Stop wasting time and get to the task at hand.

*"Quit lollygagging around and finish your homework!"*

In the early part of the 20th century, lollygagging (sometimes spelled lallygagging) was a slang word for being promiscuous. It was so popular in fact that a captain in the U.S. Navy had to issue a public warning to his sailors by announcing that "Lovemaking and lollygagging are hereby strictly forbidden. The holding of hands, osculation and constant embracing of WAVES [Women Accepted for Volunteer Emergency Service], corpsmen or civilians and sailors or any combination of male and female personnel is a violation of naval discipline."

# #61

# "Gumption"

DEFINITION

Common sense and self-reliance.

EXAMPLE

*"She'll find her way back here just fine. She's got gumption."*

FUN FACT

"Guts"
"Grit"
"Backbone"
"Good old-fashioned horse sense"

# #62

# "What in the Sam Hill?"

## DEFINITION

An expression of shock and surprise.

## EXAMPLE

*"The kitchen's on fire? What in the Sam Hill?!"*

## ORIGIN

There are many theories behind the origin of this famous phrase. Some say it can trace its roots back to Samuel W. Hill, a 19th century surveyor who primarily worked in the Keweenaw Peninsula area of Michigan. Mr. Hill had such a reputation for foul language that his own name developed into a euphemism for cussing. Another interesting theory has ties to our fair commonwealth. In 1887, Kentucky adjutant general Samuel Ewing Hill was dispatched to Pike County in order to investigate the Hatfield & McCoy feud. It is said that a few reporters printed the question "What in the Sam Hill is going on up there?" during the coverage of this story.

# #63

# "Preachin' to the Choir"

Attempting to persuade someone of an opinion that they already share with you.

*"No need to convince me that our dog needs to lose weight - you're preachin' to the choir."*

According to a recent study conducted by the Pew Research Center, 70% of Kentuckians attend church at least once per month.

# #64

# "God Love Him/ Her (or He/She Tries)"

## DEFINITION

A description of someone who doesn't have common sense.

## EXAMPLE

*"She's burned that pie the last two times she tried to cook it, but God love her. You know she tries."*

## FUN FACT

This is just another great way to saying "bless your heart"!

# #65

# "Livin' the Life of Riley"

## DEFINITION

Living an easy, luxurious life.

## EXAMPLE

*"Didn't you hear? Patrick married a wealthy woman, so now he's livin' the life of Riley!"*

## ORIGIN

This phrase originates from a popular song from the 1880s called "Is That Mr. Reilly?" Sung by Irish crooner Pat Rooney, the song features the lyrics "Well if that's Mr. Reilly they speak of so highly, well upon my soul, Reilly, you're doing quite well!"

# #66

# "Raining Like a Cow Pissin' on a Flat Rock"

## DEFINITION

A very loud, heavy rain.

## EXAMPLE

*"Then suddenly, out of nowhere, it started rainin' like a tall cow pissin' on a flat rock!"*

## SIMILAR EXPRESSIONS

"Raining cats and dogs"
"Pourin' down the rain"
"Raining pitchers"

# #67

# "Tougher Than a Pine Knot"

## DEFINITION

Very strong or hearty.

## EXAMPLE

*"You better not mess will Billy, he may not look like much but he's tougher than a pine knot."*

## FUN FACT

Kentucky is home to several different types of pine trees including the Eastern White Pine, the Shortleaf Pine and the Pitch Pine.

# #68

# "If You Can't Run with the Big Dogs, You Better Stay on the Porch"

DEFINITION

To keep up with or compete with.

EXAMPLE

*"If you get a spot on the team, you'll be expected to compete for playing time. If you can't run with the big dogs, you better stay on the porch."*

FUN FACT

With an average weight ranging between 130-220 pounds, the English Mastiff if the largest breed of dog in the world.

**This little guy could definitely
run with the big dogs!**

*Jarvis, courtesy of the Crisp Family*

# #69

# "This Ain't My First Rodeo"

## DEFINITION

I'm prepared.

## EXAMPLE

*"Don't worry about me, I remember how to drive a stick shift. This ain't my first rodeo."*

## FUN FACT

In the 1981 movie *Mommie Dearest*, the character of Joan Crawford (played by Faye Dunaway) utters the immortal line "Don't f*** with me fellas, this ain't my first time at the rodeo."

# #70

# "Even a Blind Squirrel Finds a Nut Once in a While"

---
**DEFINITION**
---

Achieving success (or being correct) through luck rather than skill.

---
**EXAMPLE**
---

*"So you finally fixed the car without breaking anything else on it? Well, I guess even a blind squirrel finds a nut once in a while."*

---
**SIMILAR EXPRESSION**
---

"Even a broken clock is right twice a day."

# #71

# "It's Comin' a Gully Washer"

A short but heavy rainfall is on its way.

*"Look at them dark clouds in the sky. Run and tell the kids that it's comin' a gully washer!"*

Elvis Presley's 1970 hit song "Kentucky Rain" was actually written by Eddie Rabbitt, who had another hit in 1980 with the song "I Love a Rainy Night."

# #72

# "Hell's Bells"

| DEFINITION |
| --- |

An exclamation of surprise or extreme frustration.

| EXAMPLE |
| --- |

*"I need to get to work by 8:30 but traffic is a mess right now. Hell's bells!"*

| SIMILAR EXPRESSIONS |
| --- |

"Hell's bells and seashells"
"Hell's bells and buckets of blood"

# #73

# "Off Like a Herd of Turtles"

## DEFINITION

Moving slowly.

## EXAMPLE

*"The kids are finally getting ready for school, but this morning they're off like a herd of turtles."*

## FUN FACT

According to the *Southern Cookbook of Fine Old Recipes*, Pendennis Turtle Soup is "the soup that made Kentucky famous."

# #74

# "You Need to Simmer Down"

# #75

# "He Don't Know Diddly Squat"

## DEFINITION

He is ignorant or dumb.

## EXAMPLE

*"Don't listen to Melvin, he don't know diddly squat about nothin'!"*

## ORIGIN

Although it's not certain, this phrase likely originates from a combination of the slang word "doodle", which means 'excrement', and "squat", which means 'defecate'.

# #76

# "I Brought You Into This World, I Can Take You Out Too"

## DEFINITION

I will beat you up or punish you severely.

## EXAMPLE

*"Don't back talk me. I brought you into this world, I can take you out too!"*

## SIMILAR EXPRESSIONS

"Keep it up and I'll cancel your birth certificate"
"You better give your heart to Jesus 'cause your butt is mine"
"I'll knock you so hard you'll see tomorrow today"

# #77

# "Enough Food to Feed Cox's Army"

## DEFINITION

A very large meal.

## EXAMPLE

*"Look at all the meat and potatoes on this table. We have enough food to feed Cox's Army!"*

## ORIGIN

In 1932, a Catholic priest named James Renshaw Cox led a pro-labor march in Washington D.C. The march consisted of 25,000 unemployed people from Pennsylvania (Cox's home state), and it made national news. There was also a protest march in 1894 in Washington D.C. led by Ohio businessman Jacob Coxey. The march, officially named the "Army of the Commonwealth in Christ," is likely where this phrase originates, as "Coxey" eventually became shortened to "Cox" over time.

**Jacob Coxey**

*courtesy of Wikipedia*

# #78

# "The Shit End of the Stick"

## DEFINITION

The worse part of a deal or transaction.

## EXAMPLE

*"I paid $900 for that lemon of a car. I thought I got a good deal, but turns out I got the shit end of the stick."*

## ORIGIN

Prior to the invention of toilet paper, cleaning up after a restroom visit was a different process. The Romans fashioned sticks that had sponges at the end of them, and when this invention made its way to American outhouses, the sponges on these sticks were often replaced with old rags. This wasn't much of an issue during the day, but if you used an outhouse in the darkness of night, it was commonplace to grab the wrong end of the stick when it was time to finish up.

# #79

# "Blind in One Eye and Can't See Out of the Other"

| DEFINITION |
| --- |

A comparison of two things that are the same.

| EXAMPLE |
| --- |

*"Don't ask me to drive. I'm blind in one eye and can't see out of the other."*

| SIMILAR EXPRESSIONS |
| --- |

"Six in one hand, half-dozen in the other"

# #80

# "Look What the Cat Drug In"

## DEFINITION

Someone who is in trouble has just entered the room.

## EXAMPLE

*"Well look what the cat drug in. It's about time you came home after being out all night!"*

## SIMILAR EXPRESSIONS

"Speak of the devil"
"Here comes trouble"

# #81

# "Actin' All Ornery"

| DEFINITION |
|---|

Grumpy or cantankerous.

| EXAMPLE |
|---|

*"Quit actin' all ornery and take your medicine!"*

| ORIGIN |
|---|

The word actually comes from "ordinary", but during the 19th century is "ornery" developed into a shortened way of describing someone who was lazy.

# #82

# "Don't Get Your Panties in a Wad"

## DEFINITION

Don't get upset over something trivial.

## EXAMPLE

*"The ice cream truck will be back in a few minutes, don't get your panties in a wad."*

## ORIGIN

This originates from the British phrase "don't get your knickers in a twist," which gained popularity in the 1960s on a television program called *The Basil Brush Show*. The phrase was augmented by Australians to "don't get your knickers in a knot" before ending up in its present-day form.

# #83

# "Egg-Suckin' Dawg"

### DEFINITION

A scoundrel or someone who is up to no good.

### EXAMPLE

*"Don't you even think about stealing a piece of that pie, you egg-suckin' dawg!"*

### ORIGIN

This phrase is attributed to a dog that will sneak into a hen house in order to steal eggs. Johnny Cash also had a novelty song called "Dirty Old Egg-Sucking Dog", which was released in 1966.

# #84

# "Courtin'"

To seek affections, date and possibly marry.

*"Froggie went a courtin' and he did ride, uh-huh."*

"Sparkin'"
"Pitchin' woo"

# #85

# "A Bee in Your Bonnet"

## DEFINITION

Something trivial that's bothering someone, a nuisance.

## EXAMPLE

*"Cathy was rude to me over coffee this morning and it's been a bee in my bonnet ever since!"*

## FUN FACT

Honeybees and bumble bees are the 2 most common types of bees in Kentucky. Bumble bees are native to our state, but honeybees are not. They were brought to America for their honey and wax.

# #86

# "Fell Out of an Ugly Tree and Hit Every Branch on the Way Down"

| DEFINITION |
|---|

A way to describe someone who is extremely unattractive.

| EXAMPLE |
|---|

*"Larry's not a very handsome fellow to say the least. He looks like he fell out of an ugly tree and hit every branch on the way down."*

| SIMILAR EXPRESSIONS |
|---|

"Beat over the head with an ugly stick"
"He'd make a freight train take a dirt road"
"He'd scare a buzzard off of a gut pile"

# #87

# "How's Your Mom'n'em?"

| DEFINITION |
|---|

How is your mother and the rest of her family?

| EXAMPLE |
|---|

*"I haven't seen your parents in ages. How's your mom'n'em?"*

| FUN FACT |
|---|

Kentucky teacher Mary Towles Sasseen Wilson invented Mother's Day in 1887 when she observed it with the pupils in her class. Six years later, she was recognized by the Kentucky Legislature as the "originator of the idea", which eventually became a national holiday in 1914.

# #88

# "Up to My Neck in Alligators"

## DEFINITION

To be preoccupied with small tasks while trying to accomplish a larger goal.

## EXAMPLE

*"I'm trying to finish this report for my boss but I'm up to my neck in alligators right now."*

## ORIGIN

This phrase comes from the old military phrase "when you're up to your armpits in alligators, it's difficult to remember that the original objective was to drain the swamp." This phrase has also been adopted as a motivational motto by various businesses looking to motivate their employees.

**Up to my neck in alligators.**

*courtesy of Wikipedia*

# #89

# "Slow Your Roll"

## DEFINITION

You need to slow down immediately.

## EXAMPLE

*"Slow your roll, Andrew, we haven't booked the vacation so don't worry about buying sunscreen yet."*

## FUN FACT

Sugar, salt, flour and shortening are all ingredients found in the recipe for Kentucky Yeast Rolls.

# #90

# "Were You Raised in a Barn?"

A question asked of someone who is uncultured or unmannered.

*"Quit eatin' that ribeye with your hands. Were you raised in a barn?!"*

The most photographed barn in Kentucky is located on Manchester Farm in Lexington. The barn is blue and white, has 3 stories, and has 4 cupolas.

# #91

# "Well If That Ain't the Pot Calling the Kettle Black"

---

### DEFINITION

Making someone aware that they are criticising someone for a fault that they have themselves.

---

### EXAMPLE

*"You're gonna get mad at Mary for smokin' cigarettes when you smoke them all the damn time? Well if that ain't the pot calling the kettle black!"*

---

### ORIGIN

The phrase first appeared in the Cervantes book *Don Quixote*, which was translated by Thomas Shelton in 1620. Shelton's passage reads "You are like what is said that the frying-pan said to the kettle, 'Avant, black-browes'."

# #92

# "If You're Gonna Hoot with the Owls You Better Soar with the Eagles"

DEFINITION

If you're going to stay up late at night you better be productive the next day.

EXAMPLE

*"It's not my fault that you went out partying last night and can't do your job this morning. If you're gonna hoot with the owls you better soar with the eagles."*

FUN FACT

Spotting an eagle in Kentucky is much easier during their migration periods and the winter season, which are between September and March. The Land Between the Lakes is a great place for sighting them!

# #93

# "Like a Bull in a China Shop"

## DEFINITION

Careless and clumsy with movement (or behavior).

## EXAMPLE

*"Bringing Martin along on this trip is going to be more trouble than it's worth. They way he cusses around the family he's like a bull in a china shop!"*

## ORIGIN

It is believed that this phrase originated in the 1834 novel *Jacob Faithful*, written by Frederick Marryat, although it may have its roots with Aesop. In one of his fables, he writes of an "ass in a pottery shop."

# #94

# "That Really Gets My Goose"

## DEFINITION

That upsets me, or that ruins my plans.

## EXAMPLE

*"I waited ten minutes for them to make my coffee, then they spilled half of it when they handed me the cup. That really gets my goose!"*

## SIMILAR EXPRESSIONS

"That gets my goat"
"That takes the cake"
"That makes my ass itch"
"That could make a preacher cuss"

# #95

# "Runnin' All Over Hell's Half Acre"

| DEFINITION |
|---|

Traveling to many other places than originally intended.

| EXAMPLE |
|---|

*"I tried looking for George's house but I didn't have the exact address. I ended up runnin' all over hell's half acre, but I finally found it!"*

| FUN FACT |
|---|

There are 21,780 square feet in a half acre.

# #96

# "Ain't Got Enough Sense to Come In Out of the Rain"

### DEFINITION

A description of someone who is stupid or lacks common sense.

### EXAMPLE

*"Jenny's pretty, but God love her she ain't got enough sense to come in out of the rain."*

### ORIGIN

"Ain't got the sense God gave a goose"
"Only got one oar in the water"

# #97

# "You're Gonna Make Me Lose My Religion"

## DEFINITION

You're going to make me lose my temper (or civility).

## EXAMPLE

*"I've told you repeatedly to quit teasing your sister. If I have to tell you one more time you're gonna make me lose my religion!"*

## FUN FACT

The song "Losing My Religion" was a big hit in 1991 for the band R.E.M.

# #98

# "She Can't Carry a Tune in a Bucket"

She's a terrible singer.

*"Her mother is a wonderful singer, but she can't carry a tune in a bucket."*

Kentucky Fried Chicken introduced selling chicken by the bucket in 1957. The idea was created by restaurant founder Colonel Harland Sanders and his first franchisee, Pete Harman. The first buckets contained 15 pieces of chicken, biscuits and a pint of gravy. Yum!

# #99

# "Your Face is Gonna Freeze Like That"

## DEFINITION

A warning to someone (typically a child) to change their facial expression.

## EXAMPLE

*"Don't give me that sour look, your face is gonna freeze like that!"*

## FUN FACT

The coldest recorded temperature in Kentucky was -37 F, which occurred in Shelbyville on January 19th, 1994. No word on if anyone's face froze that day.

# #100

# "Don't Let the Door Hit Ya Where the Good Lord Split Ya"

### DEFINITION

A sarcastic goodbye to imply that one is happy that someone is leaving.

### EXAMPLE

*"Oh, you have to be going so soon? Well don't let the door hit ya where the good Lord split ya!"*

### SIMILAR EXPRESSION

"It's been real, it's been fun, but it ain't been real fun"

*Feel free to add*

*any of your other*

*favorite Kentucky*

*expressions:*

# add to the list

☐ 101. _____

☐ 102. _____

☐ 103. _____

☐ 104. _____

☐ 105. _____

☐ 106. _____

☐ 107. _____

☐ 108. _____

☐ 109. _____

☐ 110. _____

☐ 111. _____

☐ 112. _____

☐ 113. _____

☐ 114. _____

☐ 115. _____

# add to the list

☐ 116. _____

☐ 117. _____

☐ 118. _____

☐ 119. _____

☐ 120. _____

☐ 121. _____

☐ 122. _____

☐ 123. _____

☐ 124. _____

☐ 125. _____

☐ 126. _____

☐ 127. _____

☐ 128. _____

☐ 129. _____

☐ 130. _____

# add to the list

☐ 131. _____

☐ 132. _____

☐ 133. _____

☐ 134. _____

☐ 135. _____

☐ 136. _____

☐ 137. _____

☐ 138. _____

☐ 139. _____

☐ 140. _____

☐ 141. _____

☐ 142. _____

☐ 143. _____

☐ 144. _____

☐ 145. _____

# add to the list

☐ 146. _____

☐ 147. _____

☐ 148. _____

☐ 149. _____

☐ 150. _____

☐ 151. _____

☐ 152. _____

☐ 153. _____

☐ 154. _____

☐ 155. _____

☐ 156. _____

☐ 157. _____

☐ 158. _____

☐ 159. _____

☐ 160. _____

# add to the list

- [ ] 161. _____
- [ ] 162. _____
- [ ] 163. _____
- [ ] 164. _____
- [ ] 165. _____
- [ ] 166. _____
- [ ] 167. _____
- [ ] 168. _____
- [ ] 169. _____
- [ ] 170. _____
- [ ] 171. _____
- [ ] 172. _____
- [ ] 173. _____
- [ ] 174. _____
- [ ] 175. _____

# References

It was a lot of work in researching and writing this book, so I'd like to thank some of my most valuable resources that were helpful to me along the way:

Kentucky Tourism

Wander Wisdom

The Lexington Herald Leader

Wikipedia

OnlyInYourState.com

50States.com

Movoto.com

Southern Living

The Huffington Post

Sheknows.com

Dictionary.com

Country Living

# Special Thanks

Conner Crisp

Herman Crisp

Anne Huber

Ella Huber

Holly Huber

Daniel Huber

Tasha Huber

David Sloan

John McDaniel

John Sutton

Stacey Gillespie

Kevin Kifer

Han Fan

Andrew Moore

Scott McBrayer

Kenny Rice

Scott Hall

Roger Michael

Nathan Benge

Kelly Jo Stull

Taylor Cannon

Brandon Green

Diann Brown

Sandy Pittman

Marge Crisp

**It's a Kentucky Thing - Part 2:**
**Y'all Still Wouldn't Understand**
written by
**Michael Crisp**

## MICHAEL'S BOOKS INCLUDE:

It's A Kentucky Thing: Y'all Wouldn't Understand

The Best Kentucky Trivia Book Ever

The Kentucky Bucket List: 100 Ways to
Have a Real Kentucky Experience

The Kentucky Bucket List - Part 2: 100 More Ways
to Have a Real Kentucky Experience

The Tennessee Bucket List: 100 Ways to
Have a Real Tennessee Experience

The Ohio Bucket List: 100 Ways to
Have a Real Ohio Experience

Murder in the Mountains:
The Muriel Baldridge Story

The Making of The Very Worst Thing

Blue Shirts

## MICHAEL'S FILMS INCLUDE:

The Very Worst Thing

When Happy Met Froggie

Legendary: When Baseball

Came to the Bluegrass

A Cut Above: The Legend of Larry Roberts

A Life of Its Own

The Death of Floyd Collins

Taken Too Soon: The Katelyn Markham Story

## MICHAELCRISPONLINE.COM

# about MICHAEL CRISP

Michael Crisp was born in Ann Arbor, Michigan, but moved with his family to Georgetown, Kentucky at the age of 4. Since then, he has become one of the state's most versatile and creative people.

After graduating from Georgetown College in 1991, Michael worked as a building contractor in Scott County, which developed into a passion for real estate. Michael and his wife Anne are both Realtors with RE/MAX Creative Realty, and love working with clients who are interested in buying or selling their home.

As an author, Michael has written several bestselling books, including The Kentucky Bucket List, The Best Kentucky Trivia Book Ever, It's a Kentucky Thing: Y'all Wouldn't Understand, and Murder in the Mountains: The Muriel Baldridge Story, which revisits one of the nation's most notorious cold cases. Michael is also an award-winning filmmaker, having directed several documentaries about Kentucky history. His film The Very Worst Thing, which chronicled the 1958 Floyd County (KY) school bus tragedy, won the prestigious Storyteller Award in 2010 at the Redemptive Film Festival. His other films include A Cut Above: The Legend of Larry Roberts, When Happy Met Froggie, and Legendary: When Baseball Came to the Bluegrass.

Michael lives in Georgetown with his son Conner, his wife Anne, his stepdaughter Ella, and their fur baby Jarvis.

*"A true Southerner can tell you to go to hell, and you don't figure that out for at least three days." - John Woodruff*